MW00616113

Kingdom Leadership

Leading God's Way To Fulfill Purpose

Kingdom Leadership

Leading God's Way To Fulfill Purpose

Dr. Monteic A. Sizer

Kingdom Leadership: Leading God's Way To Fulfill Purpose.

Published in Baker, Louisiana by Judah Lion Publishing

ISBN: 978-1-7356633-0-2

DEDICATION

This book is dedicated to those seeking purpose, meaning, and understanding of their leadership gifts. Unlike traditional leadership books, this book aims to connect leaders to God and His ultimate purpose. Nothing exists outside of God. All good things exist for God. God is the author of all creation and has purposed it so through His divine will and intent. It is the Kingdom Leader's choice to reconnect with the source, which is God. Doing so allows the Kingdom Leader to find true meaning, life's fulfillment, and predestined execution in the world.

Leaders have an awesome responsibility as purposed by God. It is leaders who are uniquely equipped and positioned to help meet human needs. Within this book, leaders will understand God's purpose for their lives within the context of God's principles and God's people. Additionally, leaders will come to understand better the risks and challenges of leading in a modern world. Additionally, I explore Kingdom Leadership succession, the intentional cultivation, and the development of Kingdom Leaders for God's continuous work in the earth realm.

This book is also dedicated to those who want something better out of life. It is for those who are facing life's difficulties but refuse to throw in the towel. There is hope if you will just believe and do according to God's wishes and purpose. God has predestined your steps for His glory if you trust in His processes. God will see you through.

Lastly, this book is dedicated to my four children, Kennedy, Grant, Madison, and Harrison. Know that you come from a lineage of determined, God-fearing people. You are wonderfully made and created in God's image. And through my life's ups and downs, I am your living testimony of God's gifts, grace, and mercy. You have no excuses. You have inherited a solid foundation on which to build. Make sure to choose to give God glory through your life so that your life will not be lived in vain.

TABLE OF CONTENTS

TABLE OF CONTENTS

FOREWARD

My husband, Reverend Dr. Monteic A. Sizer, embodies what it truly means to be a Kingdom Leader. From the day we met, many of our conversations were frequently surrounding the theme of his desire to see God's people live purpose-filled lives. The importance of leading God's people in a way that improves their everyday lives was paramount to him.

He is called by God and is led by God to make a significant difference in the earth realm. His life and many personal and professional accomplishments are a testament to God's grace, mercy, and favor upon his life.

Kingdom Leadership: Leading God's Way To Fulfill Purpose, is a brilliant, yet practical guide for leaders of all types. It was written for the corporate CEO, church pastor, government leader, entrepreneur, community advocate, philanthropist, and those committed to making the lives of others better.

FOREWARD

This book flows from God through my husband. God's inspiration, combined with his formal training and life experiences as a Clinical-Community Psychologist, makes this book a must-read. Additionally, his years of leading complex organizations, developing other leaders, speaking nationally, and providing consultations across the nation has given him a profound understanding of how to lead and coach other leaders.

I believe Kingdom Leadership: Leading God's Way To Fulfill Purpose, will bless you and profoundly change your life for the better. It is spiritually insightful and pushes others to find and live out God's purpose. God's people living out God's purpose is what is needed during the turbulent times in which we live.

Reverend Veronica Howard Sizer, Esq.

PREFACE

As a student of leaders, and being a leader, God gave me the eight developmental phases of Kingdom Leadership as I was getting ready to go into the office one day. They came like a flash. God said to write the steps down in outline form and then go to His Word. Being obedient to God, I did as He commanded.

The other inspiration for this book came while witnessing the 2017 Global Leadership Summit. God began to reveal what He wanted me to write and share with the world about leadership and purpose.

What follows in this book is God's insights and lessons revealed to me while studying God's Word, living life, serving thousands of others while in various leadership roles, and being obedient to God.

When a person gets to know his creator, and finally comes to know himself, then his leadership is born.

Dr. Myles Munroe

When God calls you to His will, He will place you in the deep! The deep is a place of dependency on Him! It is a place where your gifts and talents must be subservient to His will to work! Get in that deep place! Remain calm in that place! No surrender! No retreat! Just believe!

Dr. Monteic A. Sizer

INTRODUCTION

[1]In the beginning God created the heavens and the earth. [2]Now the earth was formless and empty, darkness was over the surface of the deep, and the Spirit of God was hovering over the waters.

Genesis 1:1-2

[26]Then God said, "Let us make mankind in our image, in our likeness, so that they may rule over the fish in the sea and the birds in the sky, over the livestock and all the wild animals, and over all the creatures that move along the ground."

Genesis 1:26

Ever since God created the natural, physical, and spiritual worlds from Himself, these realms naturally seek to be aligned and in harmony with God through principles that He established. All created things long for God, whether consciously or subconsciously. Anything done outside of God's will for His creation is at the root of spiritual disharmony, social problems, environmental destruction, and untold human tragedy.

Humankind's innate desire and quest in the earth realm is to search for meaning, which can only be found in God and through the work of God. In essence, humanity is seeking relationships, identity, and purpose. Thus, humankind is trying to resolve the questions of how I am to be reconciled with God, who I am concerning God, and why I am here.

An unrevealed purpose leads humanity to chase fleeting and temporal pleasures as a substitute for God's intentions and revealed plans. No amount of worldly consumption and praise can give peace or eradicate humankind's innate drive towards God, its creator.

The world is filled with brokenness and too many unrealized dreams. Nations are consumed with war and rumors of war. Too many individuals are burdened with excessive poverty and disease. Racial and ethnic conflicts polarize societies. Still, others are trapped by unconstrained moral conflicts, various forms of addiction, consumerism, power grabs, and religious strife. All of these things above are futile attempts at gaining a relationship, purpose, and meaning from life. They are a result of humanity, not knowing God and God's purpose for their lives.

For people to find peace, purpose, and fulfillment in life, it must come through communing with God and living according to God's Word, rules, and principles. God seeks to be reconciled with what He created. God is always available to His creation if sought. It is one's pursuit and obedience to God's will after many meaningless activities and disappointments that will reestablish one to their original and intended purpose.

> In essence, humanity is seeking relationships, identity, and purpose. Thus, humankind is seeking to resolve the questions of how I am to be reconciled with God, who am I in relation to God, and why am I here.

Being reconciled with God engenders peace, purpose, and meaning. It allows one to express freely and have dominion over the gifts and talents God placed within each of us. In essence, and after this symbiotic union takes place, one becomes a Kingdom Leader when the person becomes conscious of God, adheres to God's principles and rules, and expresses the gifts and talents God endowed them with for His ultimate purpose and glory. At this point, the Kingdom Leader's sole purpose for living is to please God, glorify God, and use God's gifts and talents to impact the world as intended by Him from the beginning of time.

God gives His highest created form, humanity, an equal chance of being reconciled with Him to become a

Kingdom Leader to impact the earth realm positively. To be used by God is good news for the Kingdom Leader and those positively affected by their gifts and talents.

Within this book, new insights about purposeful living through Kingdom Leadership principles will be shared. Moreover, this book will also describe the philosophical tenets of Kingdom Leadership, some of the risks that come with being a Kingdom Leader, and the cycles of Kingdom Leadership. Lastly, this book discusses Kingdom Leaders in the 21st Century, the importance of preparing for the succession of Kingdom Leaders, and concludes with overall Kingdom Leadership thoughts. The reader will have the ability to write notes and reflect on the previous topics following each chapter.

In Chapter 1, the definition and function of a Kingdom Leader are considered.

I believe that nothing happens apart from divine determination and decree. We shall never be able to escape from the doctrine of divine predestination - the doctrine that God has foreordained certain people unto eternal life.

Charles Spurgeon

Leaders must learn to live with transition. People, places, and things will change, leave, or die! Your ideas, perceptions, and desires will ebb and flow! That's life! All-natural and material things are conceived, birthed, and developed. Then they mature, decline, and pass away! If God intended for people, places, and things to remain, they could not and would not leave you! Leave you, and they must, when your purpose and assignment with them comes to an end! Celebrate the lessons learned from your experiences with them! When things end in your life, it is a sure sign that something else is about to begin. Embrace the opportunity to continue growing without them. For you see, every hand is not for yours to hold. Every burden is not yours to bear, and every relationship is not yours to keep.

Dr. Monteic A. Sizer

1

KINGDOM LEADERSHIP DEFINED

[7]Then the LORD God formed a man from the dust of the ground and breathed into his nostrils the breath of life, and the man became a living being.

Genesis 2:7

[15]The LORD God took the man and put him in the Garden of Eden to work it and take care of it. [16]And the LORD God commanded the man, "You are free to eat from any tree in the garden; [17]but you must not eat from the tree of the knowledge of good and evil, for when you eat from it you will certainly die."

Genesis 2:15-17

Kingdom Leadership is the pursuit and achievement of all that God created and purposed one to do while on earth. Thus, it is the conscious recognition that it is God who bestows one with gifts and talents to be used for God's ultimate purpose and glory. Kingdom Leaders intentionally subjugate themselves and their ambition to God's will while carrying out their predestined purpose.

Kingdom Leadership is not just a title, one's education, or position. Kingdom Leadership is not only having worldly success, money, cars, big homes, or many followers. Kingdom Leadership is about consciously pursuing and realizing God's intended purpose for one's life. It is the reason God created you. God created you for His ultimate purpose and benefit.

Everything created by God has a purpose. Inside or inherent in every created thing exists its use as decreed by God. This purpose seeks free expression and is revealed and brought out by life circumstances and being obedient to God. God is always pleased to reveal Himself to what He created.

God gave humans a choice and free will to elect to reintegrate into His original purpose. What God created is subject to God's principles and cycles, which act as perpetual regulators for God's will to come to fruition on earth and heaven. God established parallel universes to reflect His will at all times and in all realms of existence.

Nothing is outside of God. God is, and God allows what is to be.

Kingdom Leaders are born and made. Kingdom Leaders are who they were born and purposed by God to be from the beginning of time. Kingdom Leaders are made as a result of their conscious perception and free will interacting with God's established principles and cycles while being in communion with God, the source from which all things emanate.

Any person has the potential to become a Kingdom Leader because God gave all-purpose. Every person born into the world is to execute assignments explicitly determined by God. The ability to perform one's tasks entirely is predicated upon one's relationship and obedience to God.

It is the desire to be reconciled with God, being at peace in the world, domination through one's God-given gifts, and within one's earthly assignment area that separates the Kingdom Leader from the non-Kingdom Leader.

God established parallel universes to reflect His will at all times and in all realms of existence. Nothing is outside of God. God is, and God allows what is to be.

There is no insignificant purpose established by God. And God is not a respecter of person. God is concerned about His will being done on earth as it is in heaven.

God gifts, anoints, develops, guides, and protects those acting under His will and purpose. To God, fulfilling the mission for which He created humanity to solve is significant and precious. It is what humanity does relative to its God-given assignment that matters the most to God. It is truly the only thing that will last in the mind of God.

Humankind's worldly definition of significance and success cannot be used to measure or compare how God measures His creation. God measures success and importance according to humanity's obedience and execution of the assignments determined by God, while in communion with God. Thus, Kingdom Leadership can be developed and enhanced; it cannot be borrowed or purchased. God—not humans or the world—gives, assigns, and evaluates predestined purpose according to eternity.

In Chapter 2, the philosophical and metaphysical meaning of Kingdom Leadership will be addressed.

KINGDOM LEADERSHIP REFLECTIONS

KINGDOM LEADERSHIP REFLECTIONS

It has nothing to do with whether you like God's rules. It's not your kingdom. If you want to operate by your own rules, then you need to go out and create your own world. But as long as you are in God's world, where God has set the rules, you must abide by His rules or you become a rebel against His kingdom government.

Tony Evans

There are times when you must be still and understand that God is in control! You must resist the temptation to try and solve every problem and speak to every issue, quite your voice. God is working it out! When you start to have doubts, put your trust in the Lord. God will not forsake you! When you are attacked for doing what is right, place your burdens on Him. Know that God has overcome the world! Leaders, trouble comes to test your faith and build your patience. Trouble also happens so that God can reveal himself amid your storm. Again, be still and watch Him work! For you see, it is not the trials and tribulations you should be concerned about. Life happens. But instead, it is your obedience and submission to the maturation and character-building process that is most important. There is a purpose in the process! God is in control!

Dr. Monteic A. Sizer

2

KINGDOM LEADERSHIP PHILOSOPHY

[11]For I know the plans I have for you," declares the LORD, "plans to prosper you and not to harm you, plans to give you hope and a future. [12]Then you will call on me and come and pray to me, and I will listen to you. [13]You will seek me and find me when you seek me with all your heart.

Jeremiah 29:11-13

[19]When anyone hears the message about the kingdom and does not understand it, the evil one comes and snatches away what was sown in their heart. This is the seed sown along the path. [20]The seed falling on rocky

ground refers to someone who hears the word and at once receives it with joy. [21]But since they have no root, they last only a short time. When trouble or persecution comes because of the word, they quickly fall away. [22]The seed falling among the thorns refers to someone who hears the word, but the worries of this life and the deceitfulness of wealth choke the word, making it unfruitful. [23]But the seed falling on good soil refers to someone who hears the word and understands it. This is the one who produces a crop, yielding a hundred, sixty or thirty times what was sown."

Matthew 13:9-23

God created everything for His purpose. Before God created the heavens and the earth, God's infinite potentiality was contained within Himself. It was after God became conscious of Himself that differentiation began. Differentiation, our divine consciousness, established divine vibratory movements and patterns that took on many forms and purposeful functions. This differentiation is the Trinity: God the Father, the Son, and the Holy Spirit. This all-knowing Trinity, though one, permeates the visible and invisible realms of existence. It is out of this divine intelligence that both spirit and matter seek to reestablish the homeostatic union with its original potentiality, or self-contained supreme God force. God is.

God is sovereign. There is no rival. God is alpha and omega. Everything that was created, both seen and unseen, was created by God and for God's purposes. Nothing is independent of God. All God's creation has within it a natural inclination towards praising and desiring to know God.

All that has been created comes from that which has always existed. Therefore, that which was created has elements of its creator. All created things come from that divine potentiality and are subjected to the physical and spiritual principles established by God. God's established principles govern all life.

When God decided to focus conscious intent upon Himself, a divine energy spark was set in motion creating vibrational impulses of God through God for God. God's intentionality exists in visible and invisible forms. It exists in spirit and matter. God's intelligent vibrational life force takes the shape of God's intended purpose. It can be visible or not depending on the rate of God's spirit and vibrational influences interacting within realms of existence and ecosystems established by God.

The principles of the physical and spiritual worlds were established as a regulating force to give order and stability to God's creation. God's principles and cycles are the same, whether they are seen or unseen. They are the same, whether they are in heaven or on earth. They are the same, whether they are in the physical or spiritual worlds. God wills, manifests, and reveals intent through what God created.

The expression of God's spirit and principles are either base or sublime. The environment or ecosystem determines the manifested form of God's intent. It also influences how it functions, how it is perceived, how it expresses itself, how it reproduces, how it expires, and the method used to commune with God. The higher the relationship one seeks with God, the closer you must be to God.

> The principles of the physical and spiritual worlds were established as a regulating force to give order and stability to God's creation.

While aspects of God can be experienced in His natural creation, it is through the spiritual realm that Kingdom Leaders can experience God fuller and with more clarity. It is here where Kingdom Leaders begin to operate intentionally using the gifts and talents bestowed by God. Moreover, it is also at this place in God that Kingdom Leaders start to be in awe of God and can see God's hand in all that He created at various levels of existence.

In Chapter 3, the qualities and attributes of a Kingdom Leader will be explored.

KINGDOM LEADERSHIP REFLECTIONS

KINGDOM LEADERSHIP REFLECTIONS

There is no easy walk to freedom anywhere, and many of us will have to pass through the valley of the shadow of death again and again before we reach the mountaintop of our desires.

Nelson Mandela

There is a time for everything. So, what do you give when you have given it all? What is your value to the world when you have nothing to contribute to it? What will become of you? Leaders, where does your inspiration come from? Who gives you rest? Who bestows your value? Remember, the Lord is your Shepard! It is God who purposed and positioned you! It is God who knows what you need when you need it, and how you need it! Steal away and rest in God's assurances! God has promised abundance and eternal life for those who are empty for God's sake!

Dr. Monteic A. Sizer

3

KINGDOM LEADERSHIP QUALITIES

[16]Shadrach, Meshach and Abednego replied to him, "King Nebuchadnezzar, we do not need to defend ourselves before you in this matter. [17]If we are thrown into the blazing furnace, the God we serve is able to deliver us from it, and he will deliver us from Your Majesty's hand. [18]But even if he does not, we want you to know, Your Majesty, that we will not serve your gods or worship the image of gold you have set up."

Daniel 3:16-18

[9]What do workers gain from their toil? [10]I have seen the burden God has laid on the human race. [11]He has made everything beautiful in its time. He has also set

eternity in the human heart; yet no one can fathom what God has done from beginning to end. [12]I know that there is nothing better for people than to be happy and to do good while they live. [13]That each of them may eat and drink, and find satisfaction in all their toil—this is the gift of God. [14]I know that everything God does will endure forever; nothing can be added to it and nothing taken from it. God does it so that people will fear him.

Ecclesiastes 3:9-14

Kingdom Leaders are intrinsically motivated and self-determined. They believe they were created to do something significant on earth. They are continuous learners, inquisitive, and highly disciplined relative to their interests and pursuits. They are found among all races, ethnicities, socioeconomic levels, and geographical regions in the world.

Kingdom Leaders are not easily moved by crowds or peer pressure. Instead, they dance to their internal rhythm, the rhythm that God established for them. They abhor unauthentic people, places, things, and situations. They have a unique gift of sensing and reading the intentions and

Kingdom Leaders are not easily moved by crowds or peer pressure. Instead, they dance to their internal rhythm, the rhythm that God established for them.

motivations of others. Kingdom Leaders seek and desire realness and truth.

Kingdom Leaders are complex personalities. Their innate wisdom and understanding are typically beyond that of their contemporaries. While being able to display an array of appropriate emotions, Kingdom Leaders are naturally a matter of fact in their style and disposition. They are bold, purposeful, and seekers of truth.

Kingdom Leaders often incorporate facts and aspects of life when trying to explain big ideas and concepts to others relative to their purpose. Being comprehensive in their communication style allows them to be deliberate in their instructions, actions, and deeds when fulfilling God's assignment.

Kingdom Leaders tend to have very few close friends but can attract large crowds because of God's anointing and gifts that rest on them. The compassion showed toward others, and their sincere desire to assist others in knowing God and God's purpose for their lives draw them to causes and people whom God created and assigned them to engage.

Kingdom Leaders are prone to solitude and personal reflection. During these periods of introspection, Kingdom Leaders listen for God's voice and often reflect on their life's purpose and mission. Kingdom Leaders start with the end in mind, that ultimate purpose for which God created, anointed, positioned, and sent them.

They understand that life in their physical bodies is temporal and fleeting. A reuniting with God in eternity is what all Kingdom Leaders ultimately seek.

In Chapter 4, several principles that govern the disposition and purpose of Kingdom Leaders will be analyzed.

KINGDOM LEADERSHIP REFLECTIONS

KINGDOM LEADERSHIP REFLECTIONS

As you read about laws, you'll recognize that you may already practice some of them effectively. Other laws will expose weaknesses you didn't know you had. But the greater the number of laws you learn, the better leader you will become. Each law is like a tool, ready to be picked up and used to help you achieve your dreams and add value to other people. Pick up even one, and you will become a better leader. Learn them all, and people will gladly follow you.

John C. Maxwell

When you lead others, you will get scarred! You will experience danger and have to fight unnecessary battles when protecting those you lead from themselves and the tricks of the enemy. Don't become discouraged by those you lead when they don't appreciate your service or your sacrifice. For you see, you were called by God to serve! Keep your focus on Him, not those you serve. It is Him; you must ultimately give an account. Remember, it is not your battle; it is the Lord's!

Dr. Monteic A. Sizer

4

KINGDOM LEADERSHIP PRINCIPLES

[28]And we know that in all things God works for the good of those who love him, who have been called according to his purpose. [29]For those God foreknew he also predestined to be conformed to the image of his Son, that he might be the firstborn among many brothers and sisters. [30]And those he predestined, he also called; those he called, he also justified; those he justified, he also glorified.

Romans 8:28-30

[37]He answered, "The one who sowed the good seed is the Son of Man. [38]The field is the world, and the good seed stands for the people of the kingdom. The weeds are

the people of the evil one, [39]and the enemy who sows them is the devil. The harvest is the end of the age, and the harvesters are angels.

[40]"As the weeds are pulled up and burned in the fire, so it will be at the end of the age. [41]The Son of Man will send out his angels, and they will weed out of his kingdom everything that causes sin and all who do evil. [42]They will throw them into the blazing furnace, where there will be weeping and gnashing of teeth. [43]Then the righteous will shine like the sun in the kingdom of their Father. Whoever has ears, let them hear.

Matthew 13:37-43

God manifested himself by being conscious of himself. This shift of consciousness or thought set in motion purposeful, divine intent, and action. This divine intent is spirit and matter. The shape and form spirit and matter depends on the vibratory rates within the spiritual or physical world it is found in. The spiritual and physical worlds are governed by principles established by God to oversee God's creation.

Every realm of God's creation exists simultaneously and in an interconnected way. God's principles exist in heaven as they do on earth. All of God's creation has infinite depths and worlds contained within them. The ebb and flow of God's creation are done according to his will and purpose. This creation is always in a state of birth, maturation, decline, and rebirth.

The closer one gets to God, the less one can see in the natural and must rely on spiritual discernment. God's glory cannot be seen or experienced in totality. Nevertheless, that portion of God's divine purpose for humans is sufficient to enable a Kingdom Leader's purpose to be known and acted out.

Given the dynamism of God's creation and depending upon how God allows the Kingdom Leader to discern it, it will largely determine how the Kingdom Leader fulfills the purpose. This spiritual and perceptual understanding shapes and is shaped by a Kingdom Leader's interaction with God and God's creation. This symbiotic relationship governs a Kingdom Leader's life and perception of experiences en route to accomplishing a purpose.

God is omnipresent and omnipotent. God is everywhere and all-powerful at the same time. God always was and will always be. God operates at all levels and dimensions of space and time. A Kingdom Leader, while not God, can also function at multiple levels and dimensions through his or her relationship with God.

Developmentally, Kingdom Leaders vacillate and move between eight developmental phases of purpose established by God. During moments and seasons, any cyclical phase can predominate the experiences and consciousness of a Kingdom Leader. This cyclical stream of consciousness and set of experiences consumes Kingdom Leaders and propels them systematically toward God's ultimate plan for their lives. All Kingdom Leaders move through each developmental phase as directed by God according to their obedience, understanding, execution, character, and readiness to move forward.

Knowing the governing principles and phases of development, Kingdom Leaders recognize and understand how their thoughts, circumstances, and environments influence outcomes. It is through communion and relationship with God that insights are revealed and comprehended by Kingdom Leaders. Knowledge, wisdom, understanding, and correction come from God and are used to nudge Kingdom Leaders towards their ultimate, predestined purpose.

Knowledge, wisdom, understanding, and correction come from God and are used to nudge Kingdom Leaders towards their ultimate, predestined purpose.

God alone determines the purpose and timing of His will to be carried out in what God created. All creation is simultaneously interacting to fulfill a purpose predestined by God. Humanity knows chronological age and time, but God functions in and from eternity. Thus, chronological age and time are not the sole determining factors of God's principles or eight developmental phases in the life of a Kingdom Leader. God alone knows each Kingdom Leader's ultimate fate and journey as they fulfill God's purpose. However, if God purposed a Kingdom Leader to complete a task, the task must be completed as revealed and predestined. Only the Kingdom Leader can abort the fulfillment of purpose. Disobedience to God, sin, and bad character are the main obstacles to a Kingdom Leader fulfilling purpose.

Life's trials will either prepare or thwart a Kingdom Leader from achieving their preordained purpose. While life's lessons can be hard, it is up to each Kingdom Leader to choose God and trust the process God reveals. Kingdom Leaders are to use the gifts and talents God planted on the inside to avoid faltering and losing faith. Troubles do not last forever, and ultimate joy, peace, and fulfillment come from leaving the earth realm better than it was found according to God's plan.

In Chapter 5, the developmental phases Kingdom Leader experience to manifest their purpose will be explored.

KINGDOM LEADERSHIP REFLECTIONS

KINGDOM LEADERSHIP REFLECTIONS

I just want to do God's will. And he's allowed me to go to the mountain. And I've looked over, and I've seen the promised land! I may not get there with you, but I want you to know tonight that we as a people will get to the promised land.

Dr. Martin Luther King, Jr.

What have you been called to do? What problem has God gifted and purposed you to solve? For you see, it is okay to celebrate the life and legacy of people who have marched along with God's destined drumbeat for their lives. These are our witnesses and examples as we do life. Nevertheless, we do not get a pass for just celebrating and hiding behind the personal sacrifices others have made to God. Your rendition of their writings, marches, speeches, honors, and sacrifices can never authenticate their contribution again in life! God has already stamped their contribution approved! That was their moment and time with God! So, the question is, what price are you willing to pay to do God's will? What will your moment with God be? Those we honor and celebrate have already done what God called them to do! Remember, God specifically designed a rhythm and purpose for you! What will you do with your now time with Him?

Dr. Monteic A. Sizer

5

KINGDOM LEADERSHIP PHASES

[6]And this is love: that we walk in obedience to his commands. As you have heard from the beginning, his command is that you walk in love.

2 John 6

[1]If you fully obey the LORD your God and carefully follow all his commands I give you today, the LORD your God will set you high above all the nations on earth. [2]All these blessings will come on you and accompany you if you obey the LORD your God:

[3]You will be blessed in the city and blessed in the country.

Deuteronomy 28:1-3

Eight developmental phases govern the actions of a Kingdom Leader. All phases are influenced by a Kingdom Leader's relationship and obedience to God's will. Theses phases are original purpose, preparation, positioning, manifestation, sustainability, repositioning, reflection, and reunification.

All Kingdom Leaders will go through each of these distinct phases. There is no set time as to when or how it is to happen. There can even be a progression or regression depending on a Kingdom Leader's obedience to God. God has predestined the Kingdom Leader's path, according to His will.

The ultimate example for the Kingdom Leader is Jesus, being both God and man.

The ultimate example for the Kingdom Leader is Jesus, being both God and man. While Jesus knew no sin as he demonstrated how to navigate these phases successfully, he nevertheless left behind a blueprint for the Kingdom Leader, a person who is born into sin and one who must depend on God to limit sinful tendencies to fulfill a purpose.

What follows below are each of the developmental phases supported by a biblical example of that phase. These biblical Kingdom Leaders exemplify what Kingdom Leaders experience at each phase of their Kingdom journey in the earth realm.

ORIGINAL PURPOSE PHASE

God is. God is infinite intentionality. All things exist for God's glory and according to God's masterful design. Before Kingdom Leaders are manifested, they are just one thought in God's mind. God said, "Let there be," and it was. God orchestrated the material world so that God could impart His heavenly thought into what He created. Once incubated, Kingdom Leaders are forced to experience Kingdom Leadership while still void of the knowledge of it. Once birthed into God's earthly Kingdom through their mother's womb, Kingdom Leaders are forced to choose God's original purpose or that of the world.

For a biblical example of how Jeremiah demonstrates this original purpose phase, see Jeremiah 1:4-10.

[4]The word of the LORD came to me, saying,

[5]"Before I formed you in the womb I knew you, before you were born I set you apart; I appointed you as a prophet to the nations."

[6]"Alas, Sovereign LORD," I said, "I do not know how to speak; I am too young."

[7]But the LORD said to me, "Do not say, 'I am too young.' You must go to everyone I send you to and say whatever I command you. [8]Do not be afraid of them, for I am with you and will rescue you," declares the LORD.

[9]Then the LORD reached out his hand and touched my mouth and said to me, "I have put my words in your mouth. [10]See, today I appoint you over nations and kingdoms to uproot and tear down, to destroy and overthrow, to build and to plant."

PREPARATION PHASE

Although a Kingdom Leader's purpose is inside of them, it must be perfected by living life. A Kingdom Leader's thoughts, personal failures, successes, and all the countless experiences they have are designed to shape and mold them. Thus, Kingdom Leaders are being prepared and made perfect for God's purpose. God knows what to allow to ready Kingdom Leaders for His purpose and glory.

For a biblical example of how Joseph demonstrates this preparation phase, see Genesis 45:4-11.

[4]Then Joseph said to his brothers, "Come close to me." When they had done so, he said, "I am your brother Joseph, the one you sold into Egypt! [5]And now, do not be distressed and do not be angry with yourselves for selling me here, because it was to save lives that God sent me ahead of you. [6]For two years now there has been famine in the land, and for the next five years there will be no plowing and reaping. [7]But God sent me ahead of

you to preserve for you a remnant on earth and to save your lives by a great deliverance.

[8]"So then, it was not you who sent me here, but God. He made me father to Pharaoh, lord of his entire household and ruler of all Egypt. [9]Now hurry back to my father and say to him, 'This is what your son Joseph says: God has made me lord of all Egypt. Come down to me; don't delay. [10]You shall live in the region of Goshen and be near me—you, your children and grandchildren, your flocks and herds, and all you have. [11]I will provide for you there, because five years of famine are still to come. Otherwise you and your household and all who belong to you will become destitute.'

POSITIONING PHASE

For God's purpose to be done through Kingdom Leaders, God establishes the environment for His will to be done. God positions Kingdom Leaders where they need to be to be most effective and fulfill God's purpose. It is this place where God's gifts and talents, which are placed within Kingdom Leaders, become symbiotic with environmental circumstances and the physical laws that govern them.

For a biblical example of how Abraham demonstrates this positioning phase, see Genesis 12:1-7.

[1]The LORD had said to Abram, "Go from your country, your people and your father's household to the land I will show you. [2]"I will make you into a great nation, and I will bless you; I will make your name great, and you will be a blessing. [3]I will bless those who bless you, and whoever curses you I will curse; and all peoples on earth will be blessed through you." [4]So Abram went, as the LORD had told him; and Lot went with him. Abram was seventy-five years old when he set out from Harran. [5]He took his wife Sarai, his nephew Lot, all the possessions they had accumulated and the people they had acquired in Harran, and they set out for the land of Canaan, and they arrived there. [6]Abram traveled through the land as far as the site of the great tree of Moreh at Shechem. At that time the Canaanites were in the land. [7]The LORD appeared to Abram and said, "To your offspring I will give this land." So he built an altar there to the LORD, who had appeared to him.

MANIFESTATION PHASE

The manifestation phase is the principle of doing God's purpose. It is when Kingdom Leaders recognize their purpose and use their God-given talents and abilities to bring about tangible results on behalf of God for others. God's purpose is manifested in the Kingdom Leader's life in various ways and over time. Kingdom

Leaders are most productive at this stage, with their skills and abilities making room for them. Therefore, the Kingdom Leader must be sensitive to the workings and revelations of God's Holy Spirit.

For a biblical example of how Joshua demonstrates this manifestation phase, see Joshua 1:1-11.

[1]After the death of Moses the servant of the LORD, the LORD said to Joshua son of Nun, Moses' aide: [2]"Moses my servant is dead. Now then, you and all these people, get ready to cross the Jordan River into the land I am about to give to them—to the Israelites. [3]I will give you every place where you set your foot, as I promised Moses. [4]Your territory will extend from the desert to Lebanon, and from the great river, the Euphrates—all the Hittite country—to the Mediterranean Sea in the west. [5]No one will be able to stand against you all the days of your life. As I was with Moses, so I will be with you; I will never leave you nor forsake you. [6]Be strong and courageous, because you will lead these people to inherit the land I swore to their ancestors to give them.

[7]"Be strong and very courageous. Be careful to obey all the law my servant Moses gave you; do not turn from it to the right or to the left, that you may be successful wherever you go. [8]Keep this Book of the Law always on your lips; meditate on it day and night, so that you may be careful to do everything written in it. Then you will be

prosperous and successful. [9]*Have I not commanded you? Be strong and courageous. Do not be afraid; do not be discouraged, for the LORD your God will be with you wherever you go."*

[10]*So Joshua ordered the officers of the people:* [11]*"Go through the camp and tell the people, 'Get your provisions ready. Three days from now you will cross the Jordan here to go in and take possession of the land the LORD your God is giving you for your own.'"*

SUSTAINABILITY PHASE

This principle pertains to the ability to prepare people and systems to carry on what Kingdom Leaders are purposed by God to do. After Kingdom Leaders have evidenced God's purpose, it is now time for them to create ways others can reproduce on earth the glory God has allowed them to experience with Him.

For sustainability to occur, Kingdom Leaders must convey the revelation or purpose to those connected with the purpose. The Kingdom Leader is then required to train and prepare those aligned with the purpose given by God. This is done through verbal and written communication to establish systems, norms, language, and protocols for future generations.

For a biblical example of how Moses validates this sustainability phase, see Exodus 34:27-35.

[27]Then the LORD said to Moses, "Write down these words, for in accordance with these words I have made a covenant with you and with Israel." [28]Moses was there with the LORD forty days and forty nights without eating bread or drinking water. And he wrote on the tablets the words of the covenant—the Ten Commandments.

[29]When Moses came down from Mount Sinai with the two tablets of the covenant law in his hands, he was not aware that his face was radiant because he had spoken with the LORD. [30]When Aaron and all the Israelites saw Moses, his face was radiant, and they were afraid to come near him. [31]But Moses called to them; so Aaron and all the leaders of the community came back to him, and he spoke to them. [32]Afterward all the Israelites came near him, and he gave them all the commands the LORD had given him on Mount Sinai.

[33]When Moses finished speaking to them, he put a veil over his face. [34]But whenever he entered the LORD's presence to speak with him, he removed the veil until he came out. And when he came out and told the Israelites what he had been commanded, [35]they saw that his face was radiant. Then Moses would put the veil back over his face until he went in to speak with the LORD.

REPOSITIONING PHASE

After Kingdom Leaders have fulfilled their primary purposed assignment in one area of life, what else is there for them to do? This principle says that God will continue to use a Kingdom Leader's gifts and talents to bring different people to God by positioning them in ways they cannot currently imagine.

The same anointing that allowed the Kingdom Leader to fulfill one God-sized assignment will be used to build upon the Kingdom Leader's continual purpose-set established by God. And due to the Kingdom Leader's commitment and obedience to God, God is able to use and extend that anointing to reach others for the purpose of God.

For a biblical example of how Paul demonstrates this repositioning phase, see 1 Timothy 1:12-17.

[12]I thank Christ Jesus our Lord, who has given me strength, that he considered me trustworthy, appointing me to his service. [13]Even though I was once a blasphemer and a persecutor and a violent man, I was shown mercy because I acted in ignorance and unbelief. [14]The grace of our Lord was poured out on me abundantly, along with the faith and love that are in Christ Jesus.

[15]Here is a trustworthy saying that deserves full acceptance: Christ Jesus came into the world to save

sinners—of whom I am the worst. [16]But for that very reason I was shown mercy so that in me, the worst of sinners, Christ Jesus might display his immense patience as an example for those who would believe in him and receive eternal life. [17]Now to the King eternal, immortal, invisible, the only God, be honor and glory for ever and ever. Amen.

REFLECTION PHASE

This principle says that after Kingdom Leaders have used their gifts and talents for God's glory, there will come a time for them to self-reflect on their life's accomplishments and then give witness to God's purpose and promise to the next generation.

Kingdom Leaders convey their reflections in many ways. It is often done through the identification, cultivation, mentoring, and positioning of those connected to their purpose. Kingdom Leaders often convey lessons learned, things to avoid, strategies and tactics for success, and how to stay connected to God for the next level of revealed assignment and future promises.

For a biblical example of how King David validates this reflection phase, see 1 King 2:1-4.

[1] *When the time drew near for David to die, he gave a charge to Solomon his son.* [2] *" I am about to go the way of all the earth," he said. "So be strong, act like a man,* [3] *and observe what the LORD your God requires: Walk in obedience to him, and keep his decrees and commands, his laws and regulations, as written in the Law of Moses. Do this so that you may prosper in all you do and wherever you go* [4] *and that the LORD may keep his promise to me: 'If your descendants watch how they live, and if they walk faithfully before me with all their heart and soul, you will never fail to have a successor on the throne of Israel.'*

REUNIFICATION PHASE

All things come from God and will eventually return to God. This final principle says that when a Kingdom Leader's ultimate purpose, gifts, and talents have been used for God's benefit, it will be done on earth as it is in heaven, and Kingdom Leaders will be called to return to the God who sent them.

Only God knows how long the Kingdom Leader will dwell in the earth realm. Kingdom Leaders are sent because of God's ultimate purpose and will return to God according to it. God promises success relative to the accomplishment of His earthly will, and rest and everlasting communion in His heavenly realm. These assurances are promised to each Kingdom Leader.

For a biblical example of how Jesus demonstrates this reunification phase, see Luke 24:44-53.

[44]He said to them, "This is what I told you while I was still with you: Everything must be fulfilled that is written about me in the Law of Moses, the Prophets and the Psalms."

[45]Then he opened their minds so they could understand the Scriptures. [46]He told them, "This is what is written: The Messiah will suffer and rise from the dead on the third day, [47]and repentance for the forgiveness of sins will be preached in his name to all nations, beginning at Jerusalem. [48]You are witnesses of these things. [49]I am going to send you what my Father has promised; but stay in the city until you have been clothed with power from on high."

[50]When he had led them out to the vicinity of Bethany, he lifted up his hands and blessed them. [51]While he was blessing them, he left them and was taken up into heaven. [52]Then they worshiped him and returned to Jerusalem with great joy. [53]And they stayed continually at the temple, praising God.

Chapter 6 provides a brief reflection on how Kingdom Leaders can better understand their assignments and solve problems on behalf of God.

KINGDOM LEADERSHIP REFLECTIONS

KINGDOM LEADERSHIP REFLECTIONS

Destiny is not for comfort seekers. Destiny is for the daring and determined who are willing to endure some discomfort, delay gratification, and go where destiny leads.

Bishop T.D. Jakes

You will not please everyone you lead. To be successful and unmoved during this age of social media and twenty-four-hour news cycles will require you to live undeterred with rejection and disappointment. Remember, God gives His most significant assignments to those who are willing and those He can trust! It is God who will provide you peace amid your storms and attacks. He will never leave or forsake you! Additionally, the frequency and severity of your attacks are a sure sign that you are on the right track! Keep pushing! For you see, you were created and gifted by God for Him to work through you to solve some of the most significant problems in the world! If He called you to it, He would see you through it! Just keep reminding yourself, it is not your battle; it is the Lords!

Dr. Monteic A. Sizer

6

KINGDOM LEADERSHIP ASSIGNMENTS

[19]Great are your purposes and mighty are your deeds. Your eyes are open to the ways of all mankind; you reward each person according to their conduct and as their deeds deserve. [20]You performed signs and wonders in Egypt and have continued them to this day, in Israel and among all mankind, and have gained the renown that is still yours.

Jeremiah 32:19-20

[47]"Once again, the kingdom of heaven is like a net that was let down into the lake and caught all kinds of fish. [48]When it was full, the fishermen pulled it up on the shore. Then they sat down and collected the good fish in

baskets, but threw the bad away. [49]This is how it will be at the end of the age. The angels will come and separate the wicked from the righteous [50]and throw them into the blazing furnace, where there will be weeping and gnashing of teeth.

[51]"Have you understood all these things?" Jesus asked.

Matthew 13:47-51

What bothers you to the point of anger or sadness? What makes you happy? What comes easy or natural to you? What gives you energy and a sense of fulfillment and accomplishment? Who and what has caused you your greatest disappointments? Buried within these questions, you can find your purpose.

Each Kingdom Leader is created by God to solve problems on behalf of God. God endowed each Kingdom Leader with gifts and talents to be used for God's glory and to benefit others. These gifts and skills are honed or weakened, depending on the Kingdom Leader's free will and obedience to God's timing and maturational processes, as noted in the last chapter on the eight phases of Kingdom Leadership.

God is concerned with a Kingdom Leader's character and obedience to God's will and principles. God is not worried about the Kingdom Leader's wishes, comforts, or desires. God is concerned about His will and the purpose for which He created Kingdom Leaders.

God is not worried about the Kingdom Leader's wishes, comforts, or desires. God is concerned about His will and the purpose for which He created Kingdom Leaders.

God's purpose is evident in the Kingdom Leader, regardless of context. A consistent set of behavioral characteristics manifest themselves in whole or part throughout the Kingdom Leader's life.

A Kingdom Leader intuits God's instructions and acts instinctually. Sometimes this happens consciously and at other times unconsciously. The frequency, consistency, and correlation between environmental realms and circumstances begin to reveal the Kingdom Leader's pathway in the natural and spiritual worlds. These insights deepen revelatory knowledge and intensify the communion with God. When this happens, Kingdom Leaders become purpose motivated and recognize that the total of their experiences is designed for their life's work on the earth.

The Kingdom Leader has to be careful to discern God's voice as opposed to acting on their own desires and ambitions, or the desires and ambitions of others.

Failure to properly hear God's voice runs the risk of the Kingdom Leader becoming disobedient and disconnected from God. For the Kingdom Leader to become disconnected from God means an increased propensity to sin and the likelihood of heightened levels of unfulfillment.

In Chapter 7, the ways in which Kingdom Leaders can develop their leadership capabilities will be discussed

.

KINGDOM LEADERSHIP REFLECTIONS

KINGDOM LEADERSHIP REFLECTIONS

A man who stands for nothing will fall for anything.
Malcolm X

How do you say goodbye to what you love? Saying goodbye in the natural is hard. Saying goodbye in the spirit is easy. In the natural, leaders are connected to people, emotions, things, losses, and victories. In the spirit, Kingdom Leaders are concerned with God's will. Kingdom Leaders understand that life is about purpose, seasons, transitions, and timing. Essentially, Kingdom Leaders are in a constant state of being and becoming as they are being reconciled back to God. Letting go is the Kingdom Leaders way. Holding on is the natural leader's way. So, if you genuinely love something, you must change your perspective of it and let it go. What you love can't grow if you can't see its potential. Your limitations on what you love restrict, and will ultimately limit what you say you love. Leaders, how can you genuinely love what you refuse to say goodbye to? Let go and let God!

Dr. Monteic A. Sizer

7

KINGDOM LEADERSHIP ABILITIES

[105]*Your word is a lamp for my feet, a light on my path.* [106]*I have taken an oath and confirmed it, that I will follow your righteous laws.*

[107]*I have suffered much; preserve my life, Lord, according to your word.*

[108]*Accept, Lord, the willing praise of my mouth, and teach me your laws.*

[109]*Though I constantly take my life in my hands, I will not forget your law.*

[110]*The wicked have set a snare for me, but I have not strayed from your precepts.*

[111]*Your statutes are my heritage forever; they are the joy of my heart.*

[112]My heart is set on keeping your decrees to the very end.

Psalm 119:105-112

[53]When Jesus had finished these parables, he moved on from there. [54]Coming to his hometown, he began teaching the people in their synagogue, and they were amazed. "Where did this man get this wisdom and these miraculous powers?" they asked. [55]"Isn't this the carpenter's son? Isn't his mother's name Mary, and aren't his brothers James, Joseph, Simon and Judas? [56]Aren't all his sisters with us? Where then did this man get all these things?" [57]And they took offense at him. But Jesus said to them, "A prophet is not without honor except in his own town and in his own home."

Matthew 13:53-57

Individual gifts, talents, and purposes come from God. God endowed and predestined each person to be manifested from the unseen or spiritual realm into the physical or material world. God embedded divine intelligence into interlocking masculine and feminine energy to give birth to a spiritual being that is supported by God's natural and spiritual principles acting simultaneously and in multidimensional ways.

God's gifts and purposes are in every individual, experience, circumstance, environment, and developmental phase of a person's existence. This is so even when individuals who are carrying the gift and purposed assignment do not understand it.

> God's instructions for Kingdom Leaders are found in God's Word, their relationship with God, and their reverence for God.

Individuals can tap into their gifts and receive worldly accolades, yet not be fully conscious of how to attribute and use their gifts for God's purpose. Remember, God gifts and purposes us for God's glory, not the world's glory. God wants us to praise and commune with Him as we carry out God's work on earth. It becomes the conscious recognition of Who provided the gifts. It becomes one's thankfulness to the Giver of the gifts and one's obedience to the assigned purpose of the gifts. This pleases God and qualifies an individual to be a Kingdom Leader.

God's instructions for Kingdom Leaders are found in God's Word, their relationship with God, and their reverence for God. As a Kingdom Leader, you are in a relationship with God. God will reveal and give you insights into your assignment. God will create environments and circumstances to mold and shape you for your assignment. God will also assign people and resources in ways that appear supernatural to the non-Kingdom Leader.

Fresh insights will be revealed about God's interconnected systems, and realms of existence will become known to Kingdom Leaders. When this happens, all of God's people, environments, nature, and experiences begin to teach and instruct the Kingdom Leaders. The principles in the material and spiritual worlds slowly become known. Kingdom Leaders can see patterns and hear intimately from God relative to His purpose.

This understanding is not purchased, read in a book, or obtained from a sermon or leadership conference. However, God's revelation is genuinely obtained as Kingdom Leaders earnestly seek God and the purpose God created Kingdom Leaders to solve for His glory.

In Chapter 8, the challenges and risks of Kingdom Leaders will be highlighted.

KINGDOM LEADERSHIP REFLECTIONS

KINGDOM LEADERSHIP REFLECTIONS

The ultimate measure of a man is not where he stands in moments of comfort and convenience, but where he stands in times of challenge and controversy."

Dr. Martin Luther King, Jr.

Some people who start with you will not finish with you. See, it's easy for people to get caught up in the excitement and newness of a thing. They will pledge their loyalty and commitment to your God-given vision as long as they can see a benefit for themselves. They are after the gains and the glory, not the struggles and the sacrifices! So, leaders, you must be cautious of those who celebrate and pledge loyalty to you. They are sometimes the ones who will desert you when you need them most! They will refuse to sacrifice with you because they were never committed to you or your vision in the first place. They just pretended to be. Those who finish with you are the ones who are willing to go through with you! Your pain becomes their pain. Your joy becomes their joy. Your fight becomes their fight. Look for those who follow and dwell in the valley with you. These are the ones God put in your life to share your mountain-top experience!

Dr. Monteic A. Sizer

8

KINGDOM LEADERSHIP RISKS

[133]Direct my footsteps according to your word; let no sin rule over me. [134]Redeem me from human oppression, that I may obey your precepts. [135]Make your face shine on your servant and teach me your decrees.

Psalm 119:133-135

[10]The disciples came to him and asked, "Why do you speak to the people in parables?"

[11]He replied, "Because the knowledge of the secrets of the kingdom of heaven has been given to you, but not to them. [12]Whoever has will be given more, and they will have an abundance. Whoever does not have, even what

they have will be taken from them. [13]This is why I speak to them in parables:

> *"Though seeing, they do not see; though hearing, they do not hear or understand."*

[14]In them is fulfilled the prophecy of Isaiah:

> *"You will be ever hearing but never understanding; you will be ever seeing but never perceiving. [15] For this people's heart has become calloused; they hardly hear with their ears, and they have closed their eyes. Otherwise they might see with their eyes, hear with their ears, understand with their hearts and turn, and I would heal them."*

[16]But blessed are your eyes because they see, and your ears because they hear. [17]For truly I tell you, many prophets and righteous people longed to see what you see but did not see it, and to hear what you hear but did not hear it.

Matthew 13:10-16

Kingdom Leaders are driven and led by God, not the whimsical and often superficial tendencies of those who operate in the world. While understanding the world and its systems, Kingdom Leaders use their gifts to change and dominate their gifted and purposed areas.

Moreover, in every aspect of life, there will be pedagogies and competing ideologies operating for supremacy. Being in purpose and having one's steps ordered by God will engender perceptions of being different and not wanting to play by existing customs, habits, and rules. Having a disposition such as this will cause status quo seekers to openly and secretly ridicule and scandalize the Kingdom Leaders' name.

The very presence of Kingdom Leaders will cause status quo individuals discomfort and heighten their insecurities. Moreover, if they are not convincing or influential in their own right, they will seek to curry favor with those they believe have the power to stop Kingdom Leaders from manifesting their gifts. They will whisper, lie, and make the rich and powerful in society feel that Kingdom Leaders can or will ultimately threaten their sense of personal, financial, social, and existential positions in the world.

The very presence of Kingdom Leaders will cause status quo individuals discomfort and heighten their insecurities.

Those who maintain the status quo will even work against their own best interests to stop or reduce the effectiveness of Kingdom Leaders. If they cannot stop Kingdom Leaders, they will conspire and threaten people, institutions, and material objects that they think bring Kingdom Leaders comfort and joy.

Status quo individuals will accuse Kingdom Leaders of heresy, call them nonconformists, criminals, swindlers, false prophets, and insane. Kingdom Leaders must be prepared for any number of perceived negative outcomes, such as trumped-up charges, false allegations, desertion by close friends, social isolation, jail, and even physical death.

While understanding the consequences of living in purpose and for God, Kingdom Leaders draw strength and consolation from the fact that the God of the universe has them wrapped in eternity for the sacrifices they have made on His behalf in this earthly realm of existence. God promises to give the Kingdom Leader eternal rest and heavenly communion for their earthly troubles.

In Chapter 9, the benefits and rewards of being a Kingdom Leader are examined.

KINGDOM LEADERSHIP REFLECTIONS

KINGDOM LEADERSHIP REFLECTIONS

Don't ask yourself what the world needs. Ask yourself what makes you come alive, and go do that, because what the world needs is people who have come alive.

Howard Thurman

You must be honest with yourself and true to your purpose! Making a promise and not keeping it is like having faith, but no works! God requires both! God did not call you because you were perfect. God called you because you were imperfect, but willing to be made perfect in Him. Remember, God, purposed you! God knows the real you! The question is, do you know yourself? And if so, are you willing to be honest with yourself? Your past trials and tribulations are part of your purposed testimony! You can't adequately witness to others if you are not willing to be honest with yourself! The people you lead need the real you, not the pretend you!

Dr. Monteic A. Sizer

9

KINGDOM LEADERSHIP REWARDS

[12] "Look, I am coming soon! My reward is with me, and I will give to each person according to what they have done. [13] I am the Alpha and the Omega, the First and the Last, the Beginning and the End.

Revelation 22:12-13

[44] "The kingdom of heaven is like treasure hidden in a field. When a man found it, he hid it again, and then in his joy went and sold all he had and bought that field. [45] "Again, the kingdom of heaven is like a merchant looking for fine pearls. [46] When he found one of great value, he went away and sold everything he had and bought it.

Matthew 13:44-46

Kingdom Leaders have the "it factor." Anyone who encounters a Kingdom Leader will instinctually recognize their unique talents in their purposed field. Kingdom Leaders act with a sense of determined confidence and display a passion for their work. They have a profound knowledge of their purposed area of expertise and engage in it effortlessly. The expression of the Kingdom Leader's gift is when God's endowed gifts and talents uniquely converge at a predestined time, place, and purpose.

Because of the Kingdom Leaders' success in their purposed and gifted areas, they may gain material possessions and will draw lots of attention and have praise attributed to their performance. They will attract fans and followers alike. They will have deference paid to them because of their talents, especially from those for whom they have been assigned. Additionally, people will look for ways to be in their company to draw favor, learn, or grow. Many will just want to see Kingdom Leaders and their gifting on display because their curiosity and excitement have been piqued.

Still, others will gain confidence and draw strength from the persona and confidence of Kingdom Leaders. Imitation will begin, and magnificent attributes will be ascribed to the exploits of Kingdom Leaders.

> Kingdom Leaders act with a sense of determined confidence and display a passion for their work.

Kingdom Leaders draw strength from their purposed assignment. Moreover, because they are operating within their gifts and in purpose, they are drawn even closer to God. Kingdom Leaders will seek opportunities to be alone with God to hear from Him. They attribute the successes they have to God and God's purpose for their lives.

In Chapter 10, the Kingdom Leader's assignment and role in the 21st Century and beyond will be discussed.

KINGDOM LEADERSHIP REFLECTIONS

KINGDOM LEADERSHIP REFLECTIONS

What counts in life is not the mere fact that we have lived. It is what difference we have made to the lives of others that will determine the significance of the life we lead.

Nelson Mandela

What are you giving birth to? Under what conditions did you conceive your ideas? Your ideas will grow inside you for a season. They will move and kick. They will remain on the inside of you until they run out of the room and make you uncomfortable. They will cause you excruciating pain, say things you should not, and do something to abort your destiny if not released. Your vision will cause you to labor! It will cause you mental, physical, and spiritual discomfort. So, leaders, when your vision is more significant than your perceived opportunity, God will break your water and release His vision for your life if you have faith in Him! Get in position! Now, P.U.S.H. (pray until something happens).

Dr. Monteic A. Sizer

10

21ST CENTURY KINGDOM LEADERS

[3] "Lord, they have killed your prophets and torn down your altars; I am the only one left, and they are trying to kill me"? [4]And what was God's answer to him? "I have reserved for myself seven thousand who have not bowed the knee to Baal." [5]So too, at the present time there is a remnant chosen by grace. [6]And if by grace, then it cannot be based on works; if it were, grace would no longer be grace.

Romans 11:3-6

[31]He told them another parable: "The kingdom of heaven is like a mustard seed, which a man took and planted in his field. [32]Though it is the smallest of all

seeds, yet when it grows, it is the largest of garden plants and becomes a tree, so that the birds come and perch in its branches."

[33]He told them still another parable: "The kingdom of heaven is like yeast that a woman took and mixed into about sixty pound of flour until it worked all through the dough."

Matthew 13:31-33

In this age of social media, twenty-four-hour news cycles, and reality television, Kingdom Leadership is needed more than ever.

The world has generally developed an insatiable thirst for the superficial and the tantalizing. It is more about image and style than substance. It is about self-gratification rather than service to others. Furthermore, it seems to be more about what one has obtained from the world than honoring God, the one who established life and allowed individual gifts and talents to be made manifest in the world.

People cannot escape a deep desire for purpose and meaning because God placed it in all His creation. This desire has been often manipulated and substituted for the proverbial sex, drugs, and rock and roll. Materialism and overconsumption mask the deep sense for humans to feel loved, contribute meaningfully to the world, and be validated by God. The world cannot quench what it did not create; only God can do that.

There is also a moral relativism that is sweeping the world. A "do whatever feels right" self-entitlement. A sort of pseudo spiritualism based on what makes you happy, what allows you to escape responsibility for your actions, and what brings you material possessions. The more you get of this moral relativism, the emptier you will feel.

The growing popularity of pop psychology, life coaches, new-age theories, science and technology, and religion is another attempt for some to find peace, joy, and fulfillment to no real avail. Whatever the latest new thing is, it will not bring you lasting fulfillment unless God is in it. It must be of God and used for God's glory to give you any real and sustained satisfaction.

Humanity's search for meaning, combined with the pace of modern technology, is making the world a more dangerous and unstable place. Technological advances have largely outdistanced the ethical considerations needed to balance potential catastrophic uses.

While the world has become smaller due to technology, it has also become more divisive and tribal. Points of view have created us versus them, with little to no compromise between opposing viewpoints. This phenomenon will be evident in almost every social institution in the world.

From family, to political, to economic, to religious, social systems are rapidly changing and causing many to lose hope, become bitter, die prematurely from sickness and disease, and be led by those who seek power and advantage over others. This growing trend will be a recipe for mass casualties and will likely trigger a wave of authoritarian and totalitarian government formations around the world.

Nevertheless, with God, all of God's creation can be reconciled back to Him. During these trying times, God will raise a remnant of Kingdom Leaders for whom God has predestined to work on His behalf within the earth realm. These Kingdom Leaders will come from all walks of life, races, ethnicities, socioeconomic levels, and geographic places in the world. It will be this remnant that helps to establish God's Kingdom on earth as it is in heaven.

During these trying times, God will raise a remnant of Kingdom Leaders for whom God has predestined to work on His behalf within the earth realm.

Kingdom Leaders are the ones who are conscious of God and the needs around them. They are the ones who will dominate in their areas of gifting so that those around them can be served and inspired to do the same for others.

As Kingdom Leaders dominate in the areas of gift and are obedient to God's voice and direction, they will likely encounter opposition from those seeking the status quo or societal control. This opposition will not prevail and must be defeated. God is a God who does not lie or can be overcome. If God decreed it, it must come to pass.

It is the Kingdom Leaders' reconciliation to God's predestined purpose for their lives that drives and motivates them. These factors will sustain Kingdom Leaders through the trials and tribulations of life and the execution of their purpose. Because at the end of the day, the Kingdom Leader is after peace, purpose, and God's eternal embrace.

In Chapter 11, I discuss the importance of Kingdom Leadership and the role of preparing through succession other Kingdom Leaders for God's work.

KINGDOM LEADERSHIP REFLECTIONS

KINGDOM LEADERSHIP REFLECTIONS

A leader is one who knows the way, goes the way, and shows the way.

John C. Maxwell

Why are you still holding on to it? How much can you carry? To grow as a leader, you must get small. To increase your impact, you must multiply. And to extend your reach, you must delegate. Delegation is not the loss of control, but the understanding of it. So to reach, you must teach. To have, you must let go! Leaders lean not on your understanding. It is not your burden to carry! Remember, it is not your battle; it is the Lord's! Put your trust in the Lord.

Dr. Monteic A. Sizer

11

KINGDOM LEADERS AND SUCCESSION

[31]So do not worry, saying, 'What shall we eat?' or 'What shall we drink?' or 'What shall we wear?' [32]For the pagans run after all these things, and your heavenly Father knows that you need them. [33]But seek first his kingdom and his righteousness, and all these things will be given to you as well. [34]Therefore do not worry about tomorrow, for tomorrow will worry about itself. Each day has enough trouble of its own.

Matthew 6:31-34

[15]Moses said to the LORD, [16]"May the LORD, the God who gives breath to all living things, appoint someone over this community [17]to go out and come in before them,

one who will lead them out and bring them in, so the LORD's people will not be like sheep without a shepherd."

[18]So the LORD said to Moses, "Take Joshua son of Nun, a man in whom is the spirit of leadership, and lay your hand on him. [19]Have him stand before Eleazar the priest and the entire assembly and commission him in their presence. [20]Give him some of your authority so the whole Israelite community will obey him. [21]He is to stand before Eleazar the priest, who will obtain decisions for him by inquiring of the Urim before the LORD. At his command he and the entire community of the Israelites will go out, and at his command they will come in."

[22]Moses did as the LORD commanded him. He took Joshua and had him stand before Eleazar the priest and the whole assembly. [23]Then he laid his hands on him and commissioned him, as the LORD instructed through Moses.

Numbers 27:15-23

God's plans for Kingdom Leaders is for an appointed time and season. It is tied to eternity and incorporates successive Kingdom Leaders to carry it out. To do so, God provides the Kingdom Leader physical form, Godly identity, the breadth of life, position in the Kingdom, assigned purpose, helpers, and instructions to ensure willful obedience and execution. God's ultimate plan must come to pass. God uses those obedient to His will to get things done on earth and across generations.

As Kingdom Leaders do life and put the work of God's Kingdom first, they will experience trials and tribulations. They will also attract admirers, aspirants, devotees, opportunists, and critics based on their ability to dominate in their areas of gifting on behalf of God and those God intended for them to attract with their gifts and talents. God is the giver of gifts and talents. God is the one who creates the attraction in others for what the Kingdom Leader's gifts and talents offer to solve on behalf of God. God alone knows the ultimate intricacies of how this happens. Kingdom Leaders only know that they are to attract others, dominate in their areas of gifts and talents, be blessed in the spiritual and earthly realms, and be misunderstood and criticized because of their obedience to the work assigned to them by God.

Due to Kingdom Leaders dominating in their areas of gifting, God can bestow material wealth, influence, and privileges to be used to benefit the Kingdom Leader, their families, and those associated with their purpose. Kingdom Leaders attribute all achievements to God and gives first blessings to God out of obedience and dependency on Him. In so doing, Kingdom Leaders continue to sow and reap spiritual and financial benefits for the causes and purposes for which they were manifested into the world.

Kingdom Leaders are keenly aware of time and their purpose on earth. They recognize they will not dwell in the earthly realm forever. God moves Kingdom Leaders through God's developmental phases according to His time. God is the master orchestrator of events and circumstances in the life of a Kingdom Leader.

Kingdom Leaders are keenly aware of time and their purpose on earth. They recognize they will not dwell in the earthly realm forever.

Kingdom Leaders are sensitive to those God sends to assist and benefit from their work. It is the Kingdom Leader's job to enlist, train, and prepare those who demonstrate the gifts, commitment to their shared purpose, exhibits sound character and judgment, and have reverence for and shows obedience to God. God always sends successors to further the work of Kingdom Leaders. Successors are also Kingdom Leaders sent by God to fulfill their specific assignments, which are associated with their predecessor's Kingdom Leadership purpose. The successor Kingdom Leader is not to do exactly as their predecessor, but to continue the work according to God's will and the gifts and talents afforded them by God.

When Kingdom Leaders fail to enlist appropriately, train, and prepare their successors, the purpose for which God called them to will decline, but not fail. Again, God cannot fail. God's will must come to fruition. Those associated with the Kingdom Leader's original purpose will likely scatter, regress into disobedience, die unnaturally and prematurely, and some may even come to understand their assigned purpose better. Proper Kingdom succession is a matter of life, death, and purpose.

In Chapter 12, this work is concluded by summarizing key Kingdom Leadership concepts.

KINGDOM LEADERSHIP REFLECTIONS

KINGDOM LEADERSHIP REFLECTIONS

You were made by God and for God, and until you understand that, life will never make sense.

Rick Warren

What is in your hands? Are you doing what God told you to do? Leaders, to lead effectively, require discipline. It requires a singular focus on what God called and assigned you to do. Now, know that there will be distractions. Many of the distractions will come from those close to you and those not so close to you. They will often have good causes and ideas for you to invest your time in. However, the question is, is it for you to do? What is in your hands? Equally important, what is in their hands? The empty-handed always have something to say about what the leader should or should not be doing. The empty-handed! Leaders, the next time someone tells you what you should be doing, look at their hands! If their hands are empty, place some of what is in your hands in theirs.

Dr. Monteic A. Sizer

12

CONCLUSION

[14] Remember me for this, my God, and do not blot out what I have so faithfully done for the house of my God and its services.

Nehemiah 13:14

[1]In the presence of God and of Christ Jesus, who will judge the living and the dead, and in view of his appearing and his kingdom, I give you this charge: [2]Preach the word; be prepared in season and out of season; correct, rebuke and encourage—with great patience and careful instruction. [3]For the time will come when people will not put up with sound doctrine. Instead, to suit their own desires, they will gather around them a

great number of teachers to say what their itching ears want to hear. [4]They will turn their ears away from the truth and turn aside to myths. [5]But you, keep your head in all situations, endure hardship, do the work of an evangelist, discharge all the duties of your ministry.

[6]For I am already being poured out like a drink offering, and the time for my departure is near. [7]I have fought the good fight, I have finished the race, I have kept the faith. [8]Now there is in store for me the crown of righteousness, which the Lord, the righteous Judge, will award to me on that day—and not only to me, but also to all who have longed for his appearing.

2 Timothy 4:1-8

Kingdom Leadership is a choice. God created humans for God's purpose. Therefore, every person can become a Kingdom Leader if they come to know God, be obedient to God, and exercise their gifts and talents according to God.

The world needs Kingdom Leaders more than ever. The effects of poor leadership can be seen with how some leaders exercise poor stewardship over resources, the witnessing of increased poverty and disease across the world, rising racial and ethnic tensions, escalating war and violence, and the establishment of false doctrines to help justify humankind's mental, physical, and spiritual ineptness outside of God's will. There is no peace or real joy outside of God.

The ultimate answers to life and life's questions can only come from God, the creator of the heavens, the earth, and humankind. It is through relationship and communion with God that one can discover peace and revealed purpose.

There is no peace or real joy outside of God.

A critical part of a Kingdom Leader's earthly sojourn is to recognize, train, and prepare successive generations of Kingdom Leaders God sends as they work toward fulfilling purpose. When this is not adequately done, the purpose for which the Kingdom Leader was sent will decline or regress in time. The people and cause associated with the Kingdom Leader's purpose will experience a similar fate. However, God understands what He created. God will always raise and send forth a remnant to restore God's plan and promise to His creation and people. God is faithful and bound to His Word.

KINGDOM LEADERSHIP REFLECTIONS

KINGDOM LEADERSHIP REFLECTIONS

ABOUT THE AUTHOR

Leaders, you must be called, qualified, and prepared to lead others. Ambition is not leadership. Additionally, identifying and discussing problems will not be sufficient. The battles you overcame and won are your testimony. They strengthen your resolve and force you to acknowledge the true and living God. God set you apart for such a time as this. Acknowledge God in all your doings.

Reverend Dr. Monteic A. Sizer is the founding President and CEO of the Judah Lion Group and Strategies International.

Dr. Sizer agreed to serve as Executive Director of the Northeast Delta Human Services Authority, a twelve-parish regional behavioral health, addiction, prevention, and developmental disability agency. He chose to lead this organization so that his vast clinical and administrative skills could be used to help improve the lives and social systems found in Louisiana's Delta.

Dr. Sizer used his leadership and administrative gifts while serving as the President and CEO of the Louisiana Family Recovery Corps, a long-term disaster recovery organization created by former Louisiana Governor Kathleen B. Blanco and the Louisiana Legislature after Hurricane Katrina. Dr. Sizer continued to serve the citizens of Louisiana through the aftermath of Hurricanes Katrina, Rita, Gustav, and Ike.

Dr. Sizer is a thoughtful leader, consultant, and nationally recognized keynote speaker. His driving passion is to help God's people fulfill and live out purpose. Dr. Sizer's authentic, passionate, and highly energetic messages have inspired, challenged, and moved to action audiences from across the country. Dr. Sizer's firm belief is that God has given each of us gifts and talents to be used for God's glory and the betterment of others.

Dr. Sizer encourages his audiences not to let birth status, poverty, race, limited education, societal ills, family challenges, and past personal failures cause them not to seek God and His purpose for their lives. It is within God's purpose that one genuinely finds happiness, uncovers gifts, and achieves dreams.

Dr. Sizer's experiences functioning as a clinical-community psychologist, serving poor and underserved populations in educational settings, community-based mental health centers, prisons, and forensic hospitals, has given him a profound knowledge of the poor.

Some of Dr. Sizer's academic research has examined the correlation between home, school, and community influences on academic achievement, crime, and community instability. Dr. Sizer also researched ethnic identity, the causes of African American homicide, and juvenile delinquency. He is also an expert in the fields of trauma and behavioral and primary healthcare integration.

Dr. Sizer earned a Ph.D. in Clinical-Community Psychology from the University of South Carolina. He completed his clinical residency at William S. Hall Psychiatric Institute. He holds Bachelor of Science (Summa Cum Laude) degrees in Psychology and Criminal Justice from Pfeiffer College, and an Associate degree in Applied Science from Central Piedmont Community College. Dr. Sizer is also a Leadership and Political Fellow.

WORKS OF INSPIRATION

Covey, Stephen R. (1989). *The Seven Habits of Highly Effective People: Restoring the Character Ethic*. Simon & Shuster Inc.

Frankl, Victor E. (1963). *Man's Search For Meaning: An Introduction To Logotherapy.* Washington Square Press, Inc.

Greenleaf, Robert K. (2002). *Servant Leadership: A Journey Into The Nature Of Legitimate Power & Greatness.* Paulist Press.

Heifetz, Ronald A., & Linsky, Marty (2002). *Leadership on the Line: Staying Alive through the Dangers of Leading.* Harvard Business School Press.

Jakes, T. D. (2015). *Identity: Discover Who You Are And Live A Life Of Purpose.* Destiny Image.

Maxwell, John C. (1998). *The 21 Irrefutable Laws of Leadership: Follow Them and People Will Follow You.* Thomas Nelson, Inc.

Munroe, Myles (2015). *In Pursuit Of Purpose: The Key To Personal Fulfillment.* Destiny Image.

Sinek, Simon (2011). *Start With Why: How Great Leaders Inspire Everyone To Take Action*. Portfolio.

Warren, Rick (2002). *The Purpose Driven Life: What On Earth Am I Here For.* Zondervan.

Made in the USA
Columbia, SC
04 September 2020